031   Turner, Dorothy
TUR
         The man-made
         wonders of the
         world

                                    8383

DATE			

© THE BAKER & TAYLOR CO.

Educational Adviser: Lynda Snowdon
Designer: Julian Holland
Picture researcher: Stella Martin
Artist for Contents pages: Julian Holland

Photo credits:
J. Allan Cash, 12-13, 30-31; Aspect Picture
Library, 18-19; Michael Holford, 4-5, 8-9;
Alan Hutchison Library, 14-17, 24-25;
Stella Martin, 20-21; David Palmer, 28-29;
Spectrum Picture Library, 22-23; ZEFA, 6-7, 10-11, 26-27
Cover picture: Alan Hutchison Library

Dillon Press, Inc., 242 Portland Avenue South
Minneapolis, Minnesota 55415

This edition published by Dillon Press by arrangement
with Macmillan Children's Books, London, England.
© Macmillan Publishers Limited, 1983

Library of Congress Cataloging-in-Publication Data

Turner, Dorothy.
  The man-made wonders of the world.

  (International picture library)
  Summary: Photographs and brief text introduce some
man-made wonders of the world, including Venice, the
pyramids, the Taj Mahal, and the Sydney Opera House.
    1. Curiosities and wonders – Juvenile literature.
[1. Curiosities and wonders] I. Title. II. Series.
AG243.T86 1986   031'.02   86-1340
ISBN 0-87518-334-4

International Picture Library

The Man-Made Wonders of the World

Dorothy Turner

dP

DILLON PRESS, INC.
Minneapolis, Minnesota 55415

Contents

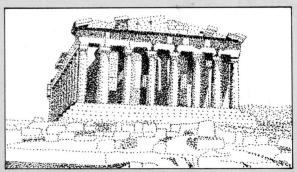

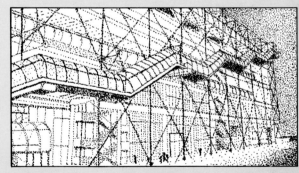

Pyramids and the Sphinx, Egypt

The strange stone creature on the right of the picture
is called the Sphinx. It has a man's head and a
lion's body. It is carved out of an enormous rock in

4

the Egyptian desert. On the left you can see the top
of a huge pyramid. The ancient Egyptians built it
out of blocks of stone. They buried their kings inside
pyramids.

Stonehenge, England

Stonehenge is a circle of very big stones. Most of
them are more than twice the height of a person.
It must have been very difficult to lift these heavy

stones into place. Nobody knows why Stonehenge was built, or who built it. It may have been an ancient temple. Here, you can see Stonehenge on a snowy winter morning.

The Parthenon, Greece
The ancient Greeks built this temple on a hill above the city of Athens. The Greeks went to the temple to worship one of their most important goddesses,

Athene. Long ago there was a huge golden statue
of the goddess inside the temple. Now the
Parthenon is in ruins. It has lost its stone roof and its
beautiful decorations are gone.

9

The Great Wall of China

The Great Wall was built many years ago to keep
out China's enemies. It is like a very long castle wall
and stretches far across the country. Soldiers used to

walk along the top to keep watch for enemies.
Today, the Great Wall is visited by many tourists.
These soldiers are not looking for enemies. They are
taking part in a film!

Pont du Gard, France

This is an aqueduct. An aqueduct is a bridge for carrying water. This one has three rows of arches, one on top of the other. It was built by the Romans

to carry fresh water to one of their cities in France.
The water came from a reservoir in the hills. It
flowed through a channel in the top row of arches.
You can see people walking along the top.

Angkor Wat, Kampuchea

This is an enormous temple. Its tall towers are built in the shape of lotus flower-buds. Long ago it was an important temple in the ancient city of Angkor.

The city was later abandoned. The people left and
the jungle began to grow over the buildings. It
remained hidden in the jungle for hundreds of years
until it was rediscovered.

15

Machu Picchu, Peru
Long ago, this was a city full of people. Nobody
knows exactly who they were, but you can see the
remains of their stone houses and temples. The

people wanted to be safe from attack, so they built
their city high in the mountains. It was very well
hidden. Nobody knew it was there until the ruins
were found about 70 years ago.

Venice, Italy

Venice is a beautiful city. It is built on islands in the sea. It has canals instead of main roads, so there are no cars. People have to travel by boat. Here, you

can see the busy water buses full of people. Can
you see the gondolas? They are the small black
boats. The "driver" pushes the gondola along with
a long pole. He is called a "gondolier."

The Taj Mahal, India

Many people think that the Taj Mahal is the most beautiful building in the world. It is made of white marble with domes on the roof and four tall towers.

An Indian ruler built it as a tomb for his wife. He and his wife are both buried inside it. As you can see, many people visit the Taj Mahal and its lovely gardens.

Neuschwanstein Castle, West Germany
This fantastic castle was built by King Ludwig II of
Bavaria. One of the things he loved most was to
build extraordinary castles. This one stands on

steep rocks in the Alps. With its tall pointed towers it looks just like a fairytale palace. It would not seem surprising if a dragon or a princess appeared in one of the windows!

The Golden Gate Bridge, San Francisco, USA
These cars and vans are crossing the Golden Gate
Bridge. It is a very long bridge which hangs high
above the sea. The road is held up by strong cables.

The cables hang between two towers. You can see
one of the towers on the right. It is a foggy day and
part of the bridge is hidden in the mist. You can just
see the sea below.

Sydney Opera House, Australia
The first thing you notice about this strange new
building is its roof. It looks like shells fitted inside
each other, or like boats turned upside down.

Inside, there are four large theaters where you can
watch films, listen to music or see operas and
plays. Sydney Opera House was very difficult and
expensive to build.

Skyscrapers, Los Angeles, USA

These are huge office towers in America. Would you like to work at the top of a skyscraper? The view from your window might look like this. The cars

down in the street look tiny. The nearest skyscraper
has five round towers. Its windows are like mirrors.
Helicopters can land on the landing-pad on the
roof of its tallest tower.

The Pompidou Center, Paris

This exciting new building has glass walls. Its steel frame and all its pipes can be seen on the outside. Inside, there are art galleries, a library and a theater.

The glass tube running up the outside looks like
a big snake. It has a moving staircase inside it to
carry people from one floor to another. The staircase
goes all the way up the outside of the building.

Places Featured in this Book